The Father's Voice

by

Elizabeth Kurangwa

THE FATHER'S VOICE

ISBN: 9781074977153

Published by:
RMPublishers
Office 1, Izabella House
24-26 Regent Place
Birmingham
B1 3NJ
www.rm-pa.org
info@rm-pa.org

CONTENTS

INTRODUCTION

I have always enjoyed reading the Bible, but I never had a specific way of reading. I have acquired some different daily devotions, but I never really went through any of them.

In 2015, we went to visit our children Tanya and Joe in America, in the state of Maryland. Tanya informed me that each year, she makes it a point that she goes through the whole Bible. This was a great challenge because when I returned to England I started reading from the beginning.

I tried to reflect on the books I had read and remembered nothing. So, I started again this time with a notebook. I wrote the scriptures that were speaking to me. As I got into it I found myself sometimes after certain scriptures I would stop and pray, sometimes I would write my thoughts and requests to the Lord. At times I felt so much excitement, like a flood rushing through when reading certain scriptures. A good example when I read about Simon Peter it was like something new. I could not keep it to myself. I phoned a couple of people shouting and dancing about Simon Bar-Jonah. So, it became more interesting with expectations. I even wrote visions that came with my reading. I found I could easily revise the scriptures that I had written. It made it easier to go over the verses that meant something to me. After reading about Simon Bar-Jonah I came to Hebrews 12 Verse 9, Apostle Paul speaks about our respect to our own Fathers yet we don't give the same to the Father of Spirit so that we can live. I felt that during my Bible study I did not need anybody to encourage me to pray, there was a feeling of warmth that I can not explain. I felt it was a personal message, I knew my father's expectations without anyone reminding me.

This new knowledge led me to see why I jumped when I read about Simon Bar-Jonah because he heard the Father's voice. It's awesome to hear the Father's voice, it is different and specific. He is the only one who calls you that way. I have written in my first book *Just As I am* that I have a gift of knowing or understanding things, but I can truly say they have nothing to do with my thinking process. Because like tongues, you speak without understanding sometimes and I write what comes just like tongues.

Like a vessel, I have to channel this information as it is given because it's not planned, it's just there like the songs. I then just write and add to the main subject like I have started dancing and jumping about Simon Bar-Jonah though I knew that for many years that moment it became new. I could not stop shouting and dancing I did not think about it something more powerful took over and I could not control it.

This is the beginning of my Bible study.

Isaiah 48 v 6 to 7: *I have made you hear new things. Things from this time, Even hidden things. And you did not know them. They were created now Not from the beginning And before this day, you have not heard them. Lest you should say [Of course I knew them]*

This verse took me to some situations in my life I took for granted but all the time the Lord was watching over me. I did not know it.

As I grew older, I never thought about how my father called me to go and do my tasks but this day as I was reading it became vivid how I used to get up so quickly when my father called my name. He called my name as if though they were two names; Elizaaaaa Bethi. The question was clear how did I hear my father's voice whilst sleeping? It was specific because only my father called me in that way. As I read through the Bible, Simon Ba-Jona's story made me realise the connection.

MY FATHER'S VOICE

My father had a farm and everyone had a duty to do some tasks. Our family was large and extended.

We lived in Plumtree then, where I grew up until I was 11. We did not have a clock in the early 1950s so we used the natural clocks i.e. the sun and the moon and the cork crows. It gave an indication of the time and my father had a specific time for planting. That is when my duties started. As soon as the maize was about to germinate, the partridges would be obviously destroying the germinating crop.

My duty was to be there before the partridges were in the field. The cork crow at dawn was the timer. The partridges could dig the whole row. I was aware that my father knew every maize crop that germinated and that is what I thought.

I was not worried to go to the fields as everyone had a task to do. I knew my duties. Each morning at dawn I woke up to my father's voice and I responded immediately regardless of the time or whether I was sleeping or awake. I am not sure how it happened but I was very sensitive to his voice and his voice alone.

I couldn't help but imagine what happened when I was fast asleep and I wondered whether his voice got to me in my sleep even when I was fast asleep. This is where my Bible study showed me: [you have to be connected to hear the Father's voice.]

My father played the role of both parents since my mother was absent. He was the only person I had a connection with.

In the darkness of dawn, I remember seeing shadows that frightened me but I still went to the fields anyway. Sometimes I waited for the shadows to pass and at other times, I just ran hoping to get away from these shadows. Screaming was not an option as then everything frightening would know where I was. So, I went in fear just hoping the sun would rise quickly as that took the fear away. I knew that when I got to the fields my father would appear from nowhere to see if the birds arrived before me. I never thought he was checking if I arrived safely but upon reflection, I think he was checking to make sure I was safe. I never told anyone that I was afraid, I just went to do the job my father expected me to do.

It is upon reflection to wonder how as a child I could hear my father's call without him shaking me or trying to use any other means to wake me up. My Father never complained that I delayed answering him. Besides the fields, I also had to clean the pig sty before going to school. After school, I had to go to the forest to look after my father's livestock. We also kept chickens that were a very special white colour, they were called white Legons, that is what my father told us. I have no idea where it came from as my father had no formal education. Am not sure if they had another name but that is what we called them.

Every afternoon we had to crush the maize to small bits using a mortar and pestle [ngiga or duri]. I was so tiny and could not cope, so I used to throw the extra maize in the bushes nearby. My step-mother complained a lot about it and when she did, I stopped altogether and she always finished the job alone.

My father never knew I couldn't do it. I was happy with lighter jobs than anything stressful. I think that is why I looked after the stock well, we really laugh a lot when I meet with my step-mother. The maize grew up in the bushes around but nobody asked. I knew my weakness. Looking after the stock was a daily task after school.

I knew if one was lost no one will rest until they were brought home. Sometimes in the forest I would feel a presence, gripped by fear of the unknown, with nowhere to run or shout but when I looked I saw nothing. There were no people around I would run in the middle of the cattle for security. It made me feel safe I had no alternative but when I look back. I remember vividly feeling so afraid even though I saw nothing though I still had the danger warning feeling in my body and sort of knew the direction of danger [something invisible but never knew what]. I remember one day I passed under a big tree running in full speed and I made the cattle run.

In my little mind, I knew I should not look up. My thoughts were: "there might be a leopard." I knew in my heart there was danger on that tree. When I got home I never told anyone because I knew no one would understand. Everything seemed to disappear overnight and would go with my father's stock with no concerns the following day. It was my duty, I knew no other way.

No one discussed anything different so I was happy to do my job as expected. My father had clear guidelines set for all he wanted to be done. There were adults who could have accompanied me or if they wanted they could have said sleep a little we will go but no one ever offered to give me a break even at Christmas and New Year's Eve. I got the best food and meat but all on my own. It was my duty and I did it as I knew my father's expectations. I then think of Samuel going to Eli because he did not know God's voice yet but Eli prepared him to hear God's voice.

When you read the Bible, you connect to His word and you can hear His voice in His messages. Samuel was not yet connected, he did not know the Father's voice and did not respond until Eli gave him advice. Eli could not take the message from God because it was between Samuel and God. Jesus said, *my sheep know my voice*. Knowing the voice, you can hear and follow also accomplishes your expected task.

One year, there was a drought. The cattle had to go to no man's land for grazing it was far from our villages [Emlageni]. So you just made a shelter from tree branches. I had to follow others after school. My father gave me the direction. There was no road therefore, you just followed cattle paths. My father told me it was far and I had to walk fast to arrive there before sunset. I had never travelled that way before so the direction was new to me.

I walked until I came to a grave with a headstone written *Griffiths Malaba*. Though I had never seen anything like it, it was different from ordinary graves. I think that was why I stood and read the headstone. I did not see any village near so I could ask if I was on the right track. Eventually, I arrived where others were before sunset. When my father wanted to know how I travelled, I told him I even saw a grave. He just said you were not to go that way. Looking back, I was lost but somehow, I got there.

Besides farm work, my father also took us to whatever entertainment was available in the late 50s and early 60s. There was a mobile cinema that came to local schools in the evenings. I remember my favourite cartoon characters *Pashure* [At the back] and *Pamberi* [In front] though I can't remember their story.

We also attended sports day which was held every year in the Town. The most memorable was the circus. We all knew that when father was holding the crank to start his Bedford you quickly rushed into the big van. It was dark green and looked like a prison guard van, it served its purpose, we all fitted in it. At the circus, we saw the lion which is our totem. Whenever anyone sent you to do something, they praised you as if you are a lion itself. As a result, you feel very proud. I think it was a way of making you do as you are asked and your reward was praise for the task done. So when we actually saw the lion my father said [nanso ke i Ngwenyama] here is the meat eater. His wives went to praise the lion.

Mavodloza - bone breaker

Eyaswela amabala - Cat with no print

Yaya bika Enkosini - Reported to the King

Thatha elikhulu -Take the big land etc

All in unison, that is 4 step mums, praising the lion as it was roaring. It was mesmerising. We were so happy to see the lion. It was personal, it was us. So, my father though not educated, he was a good caring man. Besides a strict working timetable, he provided entertainment depending on what was available at the time. A good reward for all the hard work.

Whenever the job was completed, the family was rewarded with the slaughter of a cow. We ate a lot of meat and everyone knew why we worked so hard. For me, that is where the school fees came from;

from the cattle. He explained everything and we were well rewarded at the completion of certain tasks.

Hebrews 12 :9 - *We have had our human fathers who corrected us and we paid them respect, shall we not much more readily be subjection to the Father of Spirit and live?*

This scripture made me think how much I knew to achieve goals that my father asked me to do. But I found it hard to read our Heavenly Father's word which is a guideline to achieve all that is expected of me. Jesus promised us the comforter, the Holy Spirit. As I was going through scriptures, I had a feeling of the presence of the Holy Spirit. He is always there to guide you through the Word of God. *I am Wisdom, I am standing at the door call on me and I will come in.*

I have not looked back at my life all these years but through Bible study and prayer some of my experiences came because of a certain scripture or vision. I had already written the paragraph about being frightened but saw nothing when this voice spoke. It was a voice from within me, but it was not my thought, it spoke loudly and clearly. It said [Elizabeth when you ran, I hid those things from you.

Elizabeth, sometimes I made you jump.] I had no control on my voice it just all came out loud and clear. I was not sure what was happening. As a nurse, I checked myself at work to see if I am still ok and I knew I was alright. I knew when I prayed sometimes I could have a loud conversation as if someone was telling me the right thing like verbalised prophesy [that is how I can say it]. This was new, a voice from within me. I knew I did not know this, that the Lord protected me so much in the forest. I continued to read the scriptures until I came to see why the voice, the spirit lives in us.

He can speak loudly and clearly. I experienced it for the first time. It reminded me *though we were sinners He loved us*. Though I know the scripture, here it becomes personalised and real. In John 17:21 Jesus prays that *we be one with Him as He is one with the Father*. I worried after that it was my first time to hear that voice within me but I knew it was the word of God. If Tanya had not given me the challenge to read the Bible, I would have never had heard that voice. Now I am able to encourage others to read the word of God and say the new knowledge and experience that really happened to me.

We are the temple of His Spirit. He is not far just within His temple. We are connected. If I had not read the Bible I would have missed this connection. It helped me to know He is always with me through His Holy Spirit. The voice from within me confirms He lives within us and I do not doubt. If I had not read the Bible I would not have heard this revelation that indeed when I was afraid though I could not see anything I was in danger. Only He who died on the cross saw the danger and had mercy on me. Still, I never asked the Lord to show me what I was afraid of. I would not want to know the things that came on my path in the forest. He made me not to see but run or jump. This is awesome, I never even imagined that I was truly in imminent danger. Even when I wrote in the book, *Just as I am*, I could not jump the gorge but afterwards, I was able to jump.

I always wondered how I managed when I knew I could not jump it as it was so wide. So, from mustard seed faith to great faith which is born from learning how He stood and conquered for me although I did not know. I now know how I could tell anyone I was frightened in the forest when I saw nothing but my body understood the danger and I responded by running away from danger or jumping [That is another kind of a conversation from the Lord, no voice but action.]

It is my experience in real life and my Bible study connecting me to things that happened and the Lord saying He was there to keep me safe. That made me desire to write and share what the Lord did for me before I knew him when I was just a child. He directed me when I was lost. He looked over me in every creek I crossed. He hid from my eyes every evil in the forest that came towards me. These visions and my experiences take me to certain scriptures that minister to me, freely given by the Father in Heaven. Though I was connected to my Father and knew his voice and responded immediately, I did not know the Lord's voice. I was connected by His love for sinners because He loved us even before we knew Him. I was born in sin, grew up sin but He loved me. He said harm not the little children. I was just a child doing what was expected of me. He covered me. He cared for me because His word is true [Be like little children.]As I went back to the forest I never thought of anything fearful, so I went just to do my task.

I feel my Father trusted me with his riches because though he did not know God, he knew he could trust me with all the duties he gave me. He saw something unusual but could not have known. The Lord was my Shepherd, on reflection I don't remember having any pair of shoes.

The place was infested with thorns and snakes. I was never harmed by either. It's all about my Bible study. To think the Lord even protected my little feet from thorns and I did not know it all these years. I got it through my Bible study and I see how caring our Father in Heaven is. I remember clearly when we lost our classmate. I left school on Friday and on Monday she had passed away from a thorn prick. Just a thorn prick. It was sad. Since we were young, the thought of thorns killing someone was sad but I survived even without shoes going to the forest every day walking in the darkness of dawn without shoes to the fields. If I had not done my Bible study I would not have understood how our Lord cares for each one of us in detail every day but we don't know how much like I did. If I connect the experience I have just written, when I say the Lord is my Shepherd it's alive in me, it's real. I feel something inside me He is my Shepherd.

SIMON BAR-JONAH

He was one of the chosen twelve disciples. When Jesus asked the disciples what the people say who He was, He also wanted to know what the disciples thought who He was. People related Him to great prophets like Elijah or Jeremiah. They all knew about Joseph, the carpenter. But they knew and understood that Jesus was not an ordinary man so they thought of powerful God's people. They knew He was more elevated than being a carpenter's son.

Mathew 16: 13 to 19.

Peter said you are the Christ the Son of the Living God. Jesus states that *Blessed are you Simon Bar-Jonah for blood and flesh has not revealed this to you but my Father in Heaven.*] Peter heard the voice of the Father that status raises him to be Peter the rock on which Jesus will build His church and the gates of hell shall not prevail against it.

When you hear the voice of the Father, you do not forget, it changes you. You focus on the task given to you by the voice of the Father. Peter eagerly waited for the key. As Jesus stood before Pilate, Peter followed behind while others scattered. Peter lingered behind. He was expecting to know what happens to the key he was promised. The voice of the Father kept Peter following Jesus until the cork crowed because after that it was the journey for the Lord to the cross. Peter wanted that key to shut the gates of hell but there was disconnection because their teacher was taking and carrying our sins to the cross. Only He could make that journey. Still, Peter paid attention to the conversation His Master promised him.

After Jesus resurrected, He said all power in Heaven and earth has been given to me. And in His name which is the key to open Heaven's doors was freely given. [Direct connection.] And He ascended into Heaven and that key Peter was promised came to life. He became a new man. Diseases and demons ran just from his shadow because he heard the voice of the Father. He believed the promise from his Master. He waited and followed the Father's voice and did what was expected of him. He was connected through hearing the voice of the Father. Nothing could stand between him and that connection. It was these scriptures that made me sit and write as I feel I knew what my earthly father wanted. I followed every step without questions, to all the tasks I had been given.

As I have stated, even fear could not stop me from doing the jobs my father wanted me to do. Even when I saw shadows moving, I waited for it to move away from my path and continue going into the fields to do my job as expected.

The Lord gave me a new song according to the scriptures that:

You are a shadow, OH shadows be broken in the name of Jesus because you are a shadow.

Looking at how the shadows moved away from my path as a child after this song, I know the Lord broke every shadow that came my way. I have sung the song since 2014 but now it is as though the Lord is revealing to me how He was there when I saw the shadows. It is new knowledge, I never thought the song was telling me the shadows are broken. When I sing this song after my Bible study I sing with a difference as I actually have seen shadows shift in front of me. I clearly remember talking to a shadow but now I know it was not me through His holy spirit He stood guard over me and asked the shadow what do you want? It's only by reading the scripture that I now understand that He was always there in times of trouble or danger. He took over but I always said it was me who was talking. Now I know the Glory belongs to the Good Shepherd.

We all have the key to shutting the gates of hell and they will not prevail against it. The key is His name above all names. You need to have confidence in the scripture that is connected to your situation, you can be able to do that when you read His word. When you say Jesus, the enemy will bow down. All power in Heaven and earth was given to Him. Sometimes when we disconnect from that voice we get into human philosophy and we follow flesh and blood and not the voice of the Father.

Peter, when he cut the ear of the man who had come to capture his Master, it was blood and flesh at work. He was protecting his Master. We all protect our own. Jesus said you will say I performed miracles in your name and I will say I don't know you. We need to go back to that voice that spoke to us and to follow it ignoring human philosophy.

There are so many churches today though there is one God. It's important to know the word of God so you can remain standing in His word. Sometimes in times of trouble, we seek help from churches, but you need to know the word of God to stand your ground. There is a certain level of connection to hear the Father's voice. My connection with my father was that he performed both parental roles.

Jacob had the ladder connection with our Father in Heaven. Our connection with Jesus is the Word which was in the beginning. He is the connection to the Mercy Seat. He is seated on the right hand of the Father and interceding for us always. We are connected to the Throne when we call His name through the Holy Spirit.

HEAVEN AND EARTH CONNECTED

Genesis 28: 11-22

Jacob had a dream. A ladder set up on earth. The top reached Heaven. The Angels of God ascended and descended. The greatest thing, the Lord stood above it. It is Awesome.

The Lord spoke to Jacob. He heard the voice of the LORD. When Jacob woke up he said surely the Lord is in this place and I did not know it. He says how awesome He is in this place.

When heaven and earth connect, it's awesome. Jacob received God's promises because when God spoke He promised to be with him in a strange land with strange people with strange habits. He Believed.

Jacob makes a promise that if the Lord brings him back to his land. He will give a tenth of all that the Lord gives him. After this encounter, Jacob becomes a new creation. He becomes a scientist to change Laban's stock by mixing herbs. He inherits in the foreign land Laban's stock. He becomes prophetic about all 12 of his children. He even blesses his enemies, He blessed Pharoah.

Jacob had God's protection because he never forgot how Awesome God was. Even when his family committed a crime, God always connected to Jacob as he knew the Voice of his God. He never forgot the encounter with God from the first time. It stays with you always. That is why it's important to remember your calling by the Lord like Simon Bar-Jonah without human philosophy influence.

In Genesis 34: 19, Jacob's sons Simeon and Levi slaughtered the Canaanites and the Perizzites but because Jacob kept that God-connection in his heart the Lord was there for his protection.

God says go to Bethel where I appeared to you. He could not forget. The awesome God standing above the ladder. [The ladder connection] This was Jacob's place of protection where he heard the voice of the Father.

Imagine the Cross of Calvary, once it was lifted up and grounded there was a direct heaven and earth connection. The Father, the Son and the Holy Spirit, it was awesome. The Sun withdrew its rays, the earth shook, the stones rolled away. Even the curtain of the Holiest of Holies was torn apart, it was awesome. Those who stood there said, Truly this was the son of God.

From that moment on all those that believed in Him were connected to the Holy of Hollies always as He sits on the right hand of the Father. You don't have to go to Bethel for remembrance. Everyone that believes, His spirit is with you.

In Mathew 28: 18-20 Jesus sums up His Ministry: All authority has been given to me in heaven and earth. Go make disciples of all nations. Baptize them in the name of the Father, the Son and the Holy Spirit. Teaching them to observe all things I have commanded you. Go make disciples of all nations.

It is a great conversation like: Follow me I will make you fishers of men. They heard the conversation, they stopped what they were doing and followed according to the voice and direction of the Master. I will make you fishers of men. The scriptures say the word of God will accomplish its mission, it does not have to be many words just like 'follow me.' It was sufficient for disciples to stop and follow. To know His commandments is to read His word which is His voice.

Jesus says I am with you always even to the end of the earth. This is it. I am forever connected, it's awesome. Heaven and Earth connected always believe but Jesus also said this according to Mark 11: 22-25,

Jesus answered Peter's question by saying:

- Have faith in God.
- Do not doubt.
- Believe, whatever you ask you shall receive.
- Forgive others so that your father in heaven can forgive you.
- Jesus said, follow what I have told you, this is the key to answered prayers.

He is so clear about the importance of all the above. It is a set of keys to unlock the closed doors of our lives. It is His promise, He never changes. If it is written it's final.

Jacob said where he saw the ladder was a gate to Heaven but our gate is Jesus at the Cross. Always be connected. He said I will be with you always. We should hear His word which is His voice if we want to shut the gates of hell, as He told us in the above scripture. Keep connected. He has given His word for us to follow, He says, I will be with you always.

My father gave me errands and only checked by following to make sure I was safe. I was alone, he was never there but followed afterwards to see if I was alright. His word does not change it's from everlasting to everlasting. Jesus connected us to the Father in John chapter 17. Be Glorified, it is written Jesus said so. It's a glorious connection.

In April 2015, I had just finished my afternoon prayers. I was just quiet and I saw a kangaroo in the vision with its baby in its pocket. The vision stayed for a long time, so I was looking at this kangaroo and baby in its pocket not understanding the meaning. There was no writing or anything that could make me understand this vision. It was there for a long time. There was no voice, but I knew the Man of Parables was saying something, I did not understand.

I was worried why when I had prayed and saw an animal, if it was a sheep I was not going to worry, but a kangaroo? Because it worried me I went to the Pastor of our Church. [This is connection helping me to hear the voice meant for me just as Samuel went to Eli.]

When I told him he immediately said protection? The following week, I switched on the TV and there was a documentary about Kangaroos in an Australian farm. Then I noticed that the baby kangaroo grows in that pocket connected to the mother. I then saw how the baby is protected. Though the Pastor had explained, here I was seeing with my eyes. And I then was filled with worshipping thinking I did not quite get it. I know the Pastor said protection but what I saw was engulfed in His love completely covered. If I had not got this genuine connection to our Pastor, if I had not paid attention, I would not have known how protected I was. Even writing this book would have frightened me but knowing I am doing His work, I know I am protected. He will not leave me alone even as I write. This was a conversation in the form of a vision.

I then understood how Jesus cares for us if we hear His word and believe. We get connected like baby Kangaroo. It was awesome to think He showed me how He cares. He wants to protect us continually if we hear His voice which is the word of God. Be connected. He has sent us to make disciples of everyone, we are not alone. He is there all the way. We need to hear His voice and His conversation with us. If I read Psalms 121, it's like that baby Kangaroo protection. The scripture is now real. I understand, and I believe because He taught me by a vision. The Word becomes alive. I read with awe He loves, and He cares. It is His conversation, His voice.

He says my sheep know my voice. I know now that I receive conversation from Him through songs, dreams and visions. Just like the kangaroo, I did not understand but I paid attention and consulted our Pastor. The Lord has a special way with all of us but it may be in different ways. You just need to pay attention to His voice within you. Someone recently said the period for vision is over. But I did explain to the person how the Lord showed me this vision and it was a true vision and the explanation was simple and clear [protection], that was a conversation in the form of a vision.

We cannot know the mind of God so we cannot be judging what God says to others. All God's prophets worked differently in the Old Testament but they were all God's prophets. Know your Master's voice and no one can move you from your Mustard seed-like faith to great faith. And I can say that is why in His presence no enemy makes you afraid. You stand tall in front of your enemies, never be afraid. You are connected to the Lamb of God.

When you hear His voice in any form, you will know and you are able to stand against the influence of all evil. I knew my father's voice because it was specific. When the one who called you by name before you were formed in your mother's womb, it's more specific, it's supernatural.

We are connected spiritually but we are flesh and blood. Sometimes we disconnect because of flesh and blood. And we are not aware we need that 2nd calling like Peter. To hear the voice of our Lord, Jesus is the word of God.

Let's connect Heaven-ward.

Colossians 2:8, *Beware don't let anyone cheat you through philosophy and empty deception according to tradition of man according to basic principles of the world.*

It is good for someone to teach you the word of God but to read and study the word of God gives that personal conversation with the Lord and it guides you through daily struggles with wisdom and understanding that no person can impart to you. It is living word and can vibrate through your body as you read.

GENESIS TO REVELATION IN MINUTES

THE WORD:

In the beginning, was the Word. The Word was God. Without the Word, nothing was

For God so loved the world that He gave His only begotten Son

Though there was no room in Bethlehem of Judea, He was born

As He grew up, He read the scriptures. He taught the Gospel. He taught in Synagogues. He taught in parables. He healed the sick.

At the appointed time, He was accused. He was beaten. He was spat at. Yet He uttered no word. He was accused and condemned to death. He was nailed to the cross. The cross was lifted up. As Moses lifted the serpent in the wilderness, so was the Son of man lifted up. The cross was grounded. As He died, the sun withdrew its rays. For the one on the cross was the Word from the beginning the sun could not shine on the Creator.

The earth Trembled under its creator. The one who called the earth to be the stones rolled as the darkness of our sin fell on the one who called the stones to be as the Creator died on the cross. Those who stood by acknowledged. That indeed He was the Son of God. He died and was buried. In death, He fought with the angel of Death. He defeated and rose on the third day.

He said to his disciples, all power has been given to me in Heaven and earth. In His name, we have the KEY to life. That is our connection to the Father, Jesus.

Revelation 19: 12-13, He had a name written that no one knew except himself. Verse 13 says the secret name is the Word of God. Jesus is the Word of God.

When I said in minutes I did not think of all this I just spoke it, I was singing and praying to go to my afternoon shift. I was worshipping in songs. I was singing in English and in tongues. My spirit was joyful. I could not stop. I was also dancing.

I did not stammer or struggle to speak. It was as if I knew it. I did not write it, it was not in my thought process. It was the Spirit of our Lord teaching me. I did not need to write it even as it was new, I knew it.

There was so much joy in me and so much power of the Spirit. I was definitely connected to receive this from His Throne of Mercy. I cannot forget it. It was powerful I had never experienced that. I was not reading the bible at the time it just came. As I was walking to work, I was still repeating it as if it was the Lord's prayer. So I kept saying it. But I could not look into the sky on my left side, something powerful prevented me not to turn my neck and see what was in the sky.

I was still in the Isle of Man then. When you connect to Him in Spirit, He will teach you. He is still teaching us in His word. But we all need to know His word by reading the Bible so we can stand against the evil philosophy that may come to make you disconnect [Hebrews13: 5]. I have been asking myself since why I could not look in the sky at that moment. But a few months ago, in 2018 I did not write the date down between September and October, He explained it to me.

He said with a clear voice, 'My eyes shine like the sun whoever looks into them does not live.' It shocked me, I felt weak but I was going to work I just was speechless. I never told anyone about this Voice. By Him let us continually offer the sacrifice of praise to God, that is the fruit of our lips. Giving thanks to his name.

He will answer but you need to also listen to His voice He will answer and His sheep know His voice no matter in what form the Holy Spirit, the Spirit of wisdom is within His temple.

When I came to read about Simon Bar-Jonah it was so powerful. I wanted to shout to someone and I did even as far as Zimbabwe. It was the same. Jesus is the Son of God, was the message. I knew about Simon Bar-Jonah, but now there was something powerful inside me. If I had not done my Bible study I would not know this that something powerful in the word of God can become new.

As the Spirit flows through your body, healing takes place even if you don't know it. I was on tramadol, a strong pain killer, for my left knee but I don't take it anymore. I don't know when healing took place but I knew I did not need any more pain killers.

Early this year, the Lord gave me a song in my own language ['2017]. It was about the beginning of Genesis 1:1 but I sang it in my own language. When I sang, it felt like I was running to go and tell the story of Genesis 1. I felt the Lord saying to me the Father first loved the world before He gave His Son. It reminded me of the song, Go tell it on the mountains, over the hills and everywhere.

The Father and Son are one. Jesus is the key. He humbles Himself before the Father. Jesus taught in the Lord's Prayer [Hallowed be thy Name]. For our sake, Jesus intercedes for us.

Genesis 1: 1

[Ekuqaleni kwakukhona ulizwi Ulizwi waye ngu tixo] in Ndebele

Habakkuk 2: 2 says [write it down the vision is true.]

So, I will write it down. I was lying in my bed in 2016 during the day. I saw the Lord Jesus kneeling before the Father in Heaven. I had shivers, my body shook. Afterwards, I phoned my prayer partner Fran who lives in Lincoln. I was afraid, we all agreed to kneel down and humble ourselves before the Lord. But I still find it hard to say because I judged myself. [Just as I am, who will hear me].

The truth as Habakkuk says it's a true vision, it's not mine. If it's for me to pass on for someone to humble themselves before the Lord. Ezekiel 3 says if you don't pass the message and they die in sin their blood is on the messenger's head. A voice said to me Ezekiel 3, when I read it I started writing without

judging myself but that the Lord gave me messages not only for me but for the lost sheep He is looking for or looking for disciples like Peter who will stand for Christ the Son of God without hindrance from Human philosophy.

Maybe someone will remember the voice they had forgotten. Maybe go back and study the word and the Lord will remind them just like I never looked back in my life as it was empty to me, but now I see the Lord was with me, just through my Bible study.

I thank the Lord for hiding me in the forest. My Bible study has helped me though I am not a preacher or an elder in the church. I know He cares and teaches me. His word guides me in many ways and I am confident that Jesus is the Lord yesterday, today and forever. Who so ever believes in Him is connected to all of His Glory.

I understand when King David says I will fear no evil. When you are connected, evil does not frighten you the spirit in you, the words you have kept in your heart come to life and you speak with wisdom and authority because all power and authority in heaven and earth was given to Him. He is with you always. Do not be afraid.

On a Sunday, in March 2018, the lady Pastor in our church told me she did not wish to go to work on a certain Friday. She really wanted to phone in sick because she knew she was going to deal with trouble makers. She did not want any trouble. She told me a voice spoke saying 'Try Me'. She went to work, no trouble came but laughter and joy. When I went home, I thought over it. I knew it was also meant for me. That is when I had the courage to write the above vision.

Sometimes it's just connecting with the people who may pass a word which speaks to you and you know it's your message from the Lord. That day her message was mine too. She was my connection so I wrote the vision after I had spoken to her. I listened to the voice of His word pass the message to His people, so they can come into His fold.

UNUSUAL INHERITANCE

In our native country, Zimbabwe girls don't usually get an inheritance when the father passes away. We were blessed to inherit a piece of land. The part of the land we were given originally was changed because we are girls and were given the driest part of the land which had never been used because there is no river passing through, it's very dry.

According to the records it has never been used since 1925. Most people in the family knew the land we were given was not the original offer but when I spoke with my sister that the land we were given was very dry.

As we were talking, I just saw in a vision water coming out of the pump, clear water and I said there is water. And for sure the surveyor located water and underground river so we have 2 deep wells. Now everyone is not happy. An attempt has been made to take that land from us but failed because God wanted us to have it. The Lord spoke to them to give us the land without knowing but they realised later it was against tradition.

But if God says yes who can say no? As soon as I went to see the rest of the land I saw a place with old dry trees and grass which has never been disturbed. Being a country girl, it was old and beautiful. It really looked old and rugged but very beautiful. I thought of John the Baptist and I said this place is for prayer in the wilderness. It looked so desolate, I thought of the old rugged cross. I strongly felt my spirit drawn that the Lord preserved this place for His glory. The way it looked so old and desolate but so peaceful.

Then when I was back in England, I had a dream of angels hoping on the stones in that part of our land. Then I thought we will call our land Stepping Stones. Actually, there are unusual grey stones there because it was so dense, we could not go there. In the dream, it was like the angels after travelling over the earth came there to relax. I watched the angels stepping from stone to stone. It is still a very beautiful place there is so much peace when you are there.

Because of this strong opposition, I remember some scriptures that could explain or reassure those who were not happy about the inheritance we were given. The scriptures also speak to us not to worry about what they think. Joshua 17: 3-4, the three girls came to ask the Priest Eleazar if they could inherit their father's land and they were given.

Ezekiel 45: 1 states, if you inherit land, give a portion to the Lord and it will be Holy ground. I feel we declared the place to be used for the Lord so we are not worried about the opposing forces because Jesus is the word of God. He says the wars are not ours but His. All we need is to keep His word as He is the Word. That is the connection, keeping His word.

Deuteronomy 3: 22, *You must not fear them, the Lord your God Himself fights for you.* It is through my Bible study that the scriptures become alive and speak to my situation and at the time I said for Prayer in the Wilderness I did not think we were giving a portion of our land to God but during the strife against us, I remembered there was such a scripture.

I then asked my good friend to look for the scripture and she did. Fran gave me the chapter and verse. It is this study that gave me the confidence to fight for the land and the moment I saw it, I saw Prayer in the Wilderness. I declared it for God's work without knowing. The Spirit living in you is the connection to the right decision at the right time. It is true, the Lord gives the right answer at the right time that you ask yourself afterwards, where did that come from?

This is when the Bible study becomes the Spoken word gives guidance and reassurance. The opposition for the land to be taken was so strong that even those who had suggested that we should be given were stating that they made an error.

The Lord gave me the words only He can say. I said what came into me though I did not understand what it meant and immediately peace returned. That is the Bible study helping me to speak diligently in times of trouble with immediate results I had confidence in refusing with the portion we were given because the scriptures clarified the truth to me.

My plan is to start Prayer in the Wilderness Project. People will pray where ever they want, climbing on a tree or on the rocks, just to pray. There will be a holding hall for the night. I believe it will come to pass. Imagine sitting around the fire at night in the Wilderness, Stars shining above, the fire glowing. Talking about Jesus as if He would come and explain deeper things. As He did to the two men going to Emmaus. It's a chance for some who wish to visit my beautiful country. Maybe like the shepherds, someone can find the star of their life to follow until they find Baby Jesus or find the star of your life which had disappeared. Most important to be alone with your Creator with no interruption. In a natural environment, just like John the Baptist, maybe a few bees will be humming a new song besides you. For those who are hurting maybe in this wilderness, you will be able to come out of the wilderness of your troubles and find yourself anew again. I found Elizabeth in a small Isle of Man. I found new things about me, now I am an Author, a Song writer and I do few poems HooHoo! I did not know I could do this I found Jesus in a new way He lives in me.

I thank the Lord God the Father of our Lord Jesus for giving my father knowledge and wisdom to be able to leave us huge land that we can freely use for God's purposes without fear. My father was not educated and could not read and write but he knew what he wanted. He did it by the Grace of God. My earthly Father knew we needed a break from hard work and gave us a reward to entertain us, but our Father in Heaven has greater gifts for us if we listen to his voice.

A THOROUGHFARE TO HEAVEN

A Poem:

As Jesus walked the earth He broke principalities
As He died on the cross He broke the curse of sin
For those that believe
When He died, He broke the sting of death
To those that believe
As He rose he defeated the power of death
As He ascended to Heaven
He broke powers, principalities
And kingdoms of darkness in Heavenly places
Even from the first Heaven to the 3RD Heaven
Making a thoroughfare to Heaven
For those that believe
As He sits on the Right hand of the Father
He intercedes continuously
For those that believe
The reward of those that overcome
You will arrive in Mount Zion
The city of the Living God
Heavenly Jerusalem
Into the company of Innumerable Angels
Jesus is the way the truth and life
For those that believe.
This connection is awesome forever connected.

I am grateful to Tanya who challenged me to go through the Bible. I can't remember everything but I felt His presence. I got new songs which are the Word of God. I also noted the songs the Lord gave me were actual scriptures.

I was healed during my Bible study. The pain stopped, I did not take any more pain killers. As I was reading through some scriptures as I said before, I felt excited or hot. When the Word of God goes through your body it performs what it intends to do. I went to Zimbabwe and it seemed everybody noticed I was not limping anymore. Then I realised that no one laid hands on me, it was from my Bible study.

I did not just read, I wrote what the scripture was saying to me. Just connect to the word in Faith as you go through the Word of GOD, it is Life. Paul encouraged Timothy not just to read but to study the Word of God and know the truth. It is helpful to know because you use the authority in the word without any doubt. You are sure you have the two-edged sword right in your mouth. And you have authority to shut the gates of Hell [it is written.]

You have the knowledge and you cannot perish. [My people perish because of lack of knowledge] Even

Human philosophy cannot change you if the word is in you. King David says, *Thy word have I hidden in my heart so that I cannot sin against thee.* And God loves a good heart the word of God will stay in a good heart be connected.

The Bible also tells us the reward of hearing His Voice and gives you a clear guide. I know what our Father did for us as a family. Our God has given us all a task to do depending on our calling. It's up to us to hear His guide. His call and His expectation and the Reward that awaits for us. Sometimes with Human philosophy we can just follow routines which are not His word or His voice I really understand now why He will say I don't know you even if you perfumed miracles. The question is did we use the Key? His name everything else we use, He will deny. Because all authority in Heaven and earth was given to Him. He made the thoroughfare to Heaven.

I knew I would see my Father in the field from any direction but God is always with you through the Holy Spirit. We rejoiced at seeing the lion which is only our totem what shall we say about the King of Kings, the Lion of Judah? He covers us when we are under attack as I was in the forest. He prayed to the

Father to keep us safe on this earth and still intercedes for us without ceasing. He deserves our praise always.

I could not impart this vision when I saw our Lord humbling Himself before the Father for our sake. It made me so weak. I wish I could share it so we can understand the Love of Jesus Christ. While they crucified Him, He said forgive them Father. He still says it to the Father for our sake, Let us make disciples of everyone for His glory, not our own Glory.

Revelation 3:20, Behold I stand at the door and knock. If anyone hears my voice and opens the door, I will come to him. Will dine with him and him with me. Be connected by His word. It reassures me that when I heard myself talking about [Elizabeth I hid these things from you], it was my Lord through His HOLY spirit.

In the book of Ecclesiastes, the preacher studies the life of man. He looks at his generation and the generations before him and generations to come and makes a conclusion:

Chapter 12:13 Fear God and keep his commandments, For this is the whole duty of man.

Conclusion advantages of knowing His word makes you hear His voice and follow His call with confidence knowing His word is living Word.

Besides hearing the voice, it's important to pay attention to the message of the voice. Though I heard my father's voice there are two occasions that I failed the task. I was sent to go and ask for a rack from the neighbouring farm. I had never seen it, I did not know what it was used for. My father did not explain he just said go and ask them if they can lend us a rack. When I got to the neighbour's farm I said I have been sent to ask for a cheque that was in the early sixties. They said a cheque is something found at the post office. I can't remember if I used the word or I had forgotten both words but I know my father went to buy one with no incidence of my doing wrong. I then knew what a rack was.

The second incident was when we had a school concert. My father gave me half a crown [two shillings and sixpence] it was one coin. He told me to bring back sixpence. But I saw that there was so much money in the bag where the money came from so I used it. Father made it clear he wanted the money so I think I found it but I can't remember where but he meant what he said.

He did not explain budgeting, and I think now that is what he was teaching me. He was also teaching me to follow instruction and only take what I have been given.

Some times you may be like me because the farm was a distance. I forgot, and there will be someone the Holy Spirit or a Pastor who can help us to remember His instruction to us. There is a lesson that is not clear if you pay attention to the word of God. The word is there to guide us and help us pay attention to the Voice of our Shepherd. Samuel had Eli and Saul of Tarshish, though he was certified to kill Believers in Christ when He met him on his journey to kill believers he knew it was the Lord.

As I had finished writing the Lord explained a few things that I did not know when I wrote *Just as I am*. I knew the gorge in the chapter about my encounter in the wilderness was wide and very deep. I knew I should not have jumped because I had realised I couldn't. The Voice was clear [Elizabeth I made you Jump. In that darkness where I was born, He loved me. My father protected me by not explaining my visions and dreams in case I started big trouble by talking about them to others.

My father waited his lifetime. To sum up my visions and dreams in a few words which spoke volumes [don't you think I also would like to see the things you see]. He passed on before the way was opened for me to know most of it was the Lord my saviour guarding me jealously against the plans of His enemies.

I did not know the Lord shut down my memory so that yesterday was forgotten and was ready to do my task without fear the following day. After writing this book the Lord has spoken to explain things beyond my imagination though my topic is about hearing His voice. He made it practical by telling me the things I did not know and only He could know, to me they were Miracles. This was in an audible voice and calling my name, I mean the one who was in the beginning, calling you by name? He wants all His sheep to hear His voice and follow His footsteps He is always there. He never lives His sheep alone. I have had conversations while writing this book that I can't even explain it. About my work, it shook me up to now it makes me shiver. I realise He was there every day at work with me. He knows how I work. He is the Word when He speaks few words you understand the whole topic. *Just as I am*, I shiver a lot when I think in a short time He explained a lot, what if we all read His word and He communicates with all of us. Paying attention and listening, it's amazing. He cares for us in every department of our lives.

To conclude my Bible study, I feel the Song by Jarrod Cooper sums all my feelings, King of Kings Majesty.